P9-BIW-798

Nature's Children

FLIES

James Martin

GROLIER

FACTS IN BRIEF

Classification of Flies

Class: *Insecta* (insects)
Order: *Diptera* (true flies)
Species: There are at least 200,000 species of flies

World distribution.   Flies live all around the world except at the polar icecaps.

Habitat.   On land and in fresh waters everywhere; absent from the ocean, though a few species live in rock pools.

Distinctive physical characteristics.   Young are wormlike maggots, adults have one pair of wings, with the hind pair reduced to tiny halteres.

Habits.   Young often live underground, inside plants, or inside food like living or dead animals or dung; adults fly freely.

Diet.   Young may eat decaying animal or plant material, leaves and roots, dead animals, or catch other tiny creatures. Some adults feed on sweet liquids like nectar. Some drink blood. Some are hunters. Many live on or in other living creatures.

© 2004 The Brown Reference Group plc
Printed and bound in U.S.A.
Edited by John Farndon and Angela Koo

Published by:

An imprint of Scholastic Library Publishing Old Sherman Turnpike, Danbury, Connecticut 06816

Library of Congress Cataloging-in-Publication Data
Martin, James W. R.
    Flies / James W. R. Martin.
        p. cm. — (Nature's children)
    Includes index.
    Summary: Describes the physical characteristics, habits, and natural environment of flies.
    ISBN 0-7172-5957-9 (set)   ISBN 0-7172-5964-1
    1. Flies—Juvenile literature. [1. Flies.] I. Title. II. Series.

QL533.2.M27 2004
595.77—dc22

2003049168

Contents

Does a fly buzzing against a window annoy you? Before you try to squash it, stop and take a closer look. Flies are truly amazing insects. With their great agility they make flying through the air look easy.

Some flies are of great importance to people since they help plants produce seeds and fruits, while others clean up dead animals and dung. Other flies are not so helpful, and some carry deadly diseases from person to person. Flies have many enemies, from spiders to birds and even some plants. But they can sometimes fool them by pretending to be another type of insect altogether! Some flies even turn the tables and catch other animals for food.

Flies suck up their food, and they especially like sucking on sweet food, such as this cake.

What Is a Fly?

People use the word "fly" when they are talking about many different types of insects, such as a dragonfly, mayfly, or butterfly. But to a scientist who studies insects, "fly" has a much more precise meaning. It refers only to a particular group of insects called the Diptera, or true flies.

You can easily tell a fly from any other type of insect by looking closely at its wings. Most insects have four wings to fly, but flies and beetles get by with just two. Beetles have a pair of hard wing cases covering their wings that flies lack. So, if you find a mystery insect with just two wings and no wing cases, you will know that you have found a fly!

A few kinds of flies do not have any wings at all, but the rest all have just two wings. In other ways, though, flies are incredibly diverse, and scientists think there are more than 200,000 different types in the world today.

Flies are easy to recognize because they have only two wings, not four like other flying insects.

Where Do Flies Live?

You might only notice a fly when it annoys you by landing on your food or by buzzing noisily against a window pane. But take a look in your backyard or in a local wood in spring or summer, and you will see that flies are everywhere. Some flies can be seen mainly in nasty places like on cowpats or near dead animals. Although people don't like these things, flies love them. They provide a great spot to lay eggs, and their young will munch away at the rotting dung or flesh.

The young of insects such as flies are called larvae. Fly larvae are usually harder to find than adult flies. They hide away out of the light so enemies cannot find and eat them. They also live in very different places than the flying adults. That helps more survive to adulthood, since they do not have to compete with the adults for food. And it explains why larvae and adult flies look so different: because they are adapted to live in different places and to eat different things.

Opposite page: Flies can often be seen around rotting meat and vegetables or on dung, like these.

9

Shapes and Sizes

To an expert the larvae of most flies look very different. But they all have no legs and look like small worms. Adult flies, however, come in an extraordinary range of shapes and sizes. Flies' names often give away their most obvious features; there are long-legged flies, broad-headed flies, thick-headed flies, and even stalk-eyed flies.

Some flies are tiny. Some midges are only 0.04 inches (1 millimeter) long. These insects drink the blood of other animals, including people, but they are so small that even a gentle breeze will blow them away from their intended victims. By contrast, mydas flies are true giants of the insect world. These monsters measure up to 3 inches (8 centimeters) long, while some crane flies have massive wingspans that can reach 4 inches (10 centimeters) across.

It looks as if this fly has two big eyes. In fact, each "eye" is made of thousands of little eyelets.

Strange Senses

When a housefly lands on something tasty, it walks on it for a time before it starts to feed. That is because flies taste food through their feet! Flies also see in a different way than people do. They have compound eyes made up of thousands of separate lenses. They allow a fly to see the world around it as a pattern of light and dark dots. Compound eyes are excellent for spotting a slight movement very quickly. Flies' bodies are also covered with tiny hairs that track the movement of air around them. These features combine to help flies swiftly escape from an enemy, such as an angry person trying clumsily to swat them with a newspaper!

For some flies other senses are just as important. The antennae of male mosquitoes, for example, are used to detect sound. They can pick up the sounds made by the beating wings of a female mosquito, allowing these flies to find each other in the dark.

Fabulous Fliers

Flies are amazingly agile in the air. Many can fly backward and sideways, and can change direction quickly. A fly's wing is shaped so that air moves across it in a way that sucks the wing upward. That gives the insect the lift it needs to stay aloft, but it must beat its wings very quickly. Hover flies beat their wings around 350 times each second. That helps them hover beside a flower as they drink its nectar. Impressive, but some way short of the champion insect wing beater—a type of midge that can flap its wings more than 1,000 times each second!

Flies are also among the fastest of all insect fliers. Scientists have clocked one type of botfly at 25 miles an hour (40 kilometers an hour), and some crane flies may be able to travel even faster than that.

If you look closely, you can just see two tiny little knobs at this fly's wing roots. They are the halteres.

Keeping Balanced

Flies use two wings to zoom through the air. Most other insects, however, like butterflies, bees, and wasps, have four wings. The ancient ancestors of flies had four wings too. Over millions of years flies' second pair of wings changed into a pair of tiny rods shaped like chicken drumsticks. They are called halteres, and they are very important, since they help a fly keep its balance as it flies along. The halteres waggle from side to side as the fly moves through the air. They help the fly know if it begins to drift off course.

Getting a Mate

Opposite page:
Midges are tiny insects. But when they are ready to mate, the males and females gather in huge swarms like this.

When it is time to breed, many male flies form swarms. Midges form swarms over a landmark like a tree branch or a fence post. If a female midge visits the swarm, the males compete for her—often it is the smaller, more agile males that win. In a few types of flies the females form swarms instead. In one type of dance fly, for example, the males present the females with the gift of a dead insect. The gift is worth battling for, so the females form swarms in which they compete for the males with the best presents.

Other flies do not swarm but compete all the same. Stalk-eyed flies have long horns on their heads, with their eyes at the tip. Competing males square off to face each other, but the females usually go for the males with the longest horns.

Getting Bigger

You might have seen some wriggling maggots in the bottom of a trashcan or on the end of a fisher's hook. But did you know that these weird, wormlike animals are actually the larvae, or young, of many larger kinds of fly, like houseflies? Adult flies lay eggs near things that the young flies like to eat. When these eggs hatch, the little maggots pop out.

Maggots eat like crazy. They must grow as quickly as they can. But maggots and other young insects are very different from people, since their skins are very tough and do not stretch. So, in order to grow, a maggot must shed its skin, or molt. Once it has molted, the maggot swiftly expands its body before its new skin hardens.

Flies often lay their eggs on rotting meat so the maggots have plenty of food to eat when they hatch.

Becoming an Adult

After a maggot has eaten and eaten, and molted several times, it is ready to become an adult. You might wonder how a wormlike maggot could possibly become a graceful, flying adult fly. To make this massive change, a maggot becomes a pupa. Some maggots first shed their skin one last time, though. Then they settle down inside the dead skin to become a pupa.

The fly cannot move while it is a pupa, so it first finds a safe, sheltered spot. The fly may stay resting as a pupa through the cold winter months. Then, in the spring bits of the maggot's body break down, while adult body parts like wings, legs, and eyes grow from tiny buds. When the change is complete, the adult fly breaks through the dead skin. It waits for its wings to harden before starting to fly.

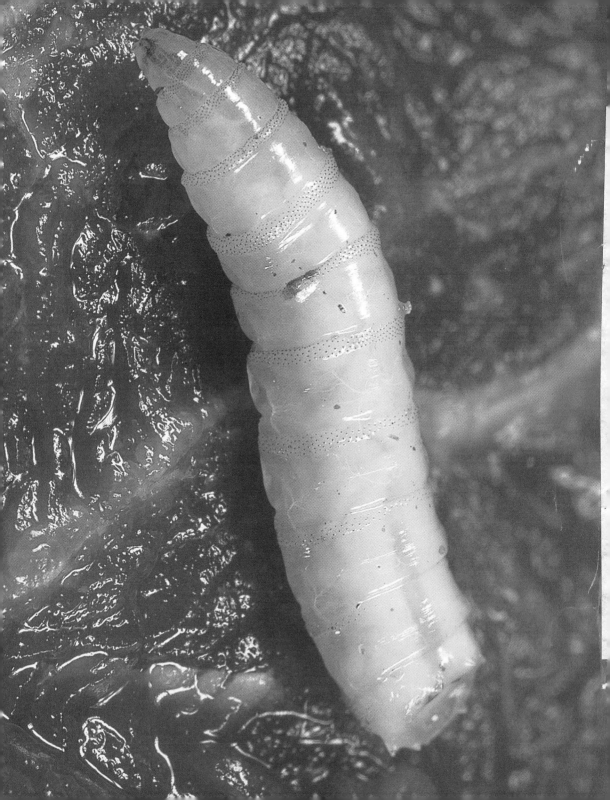

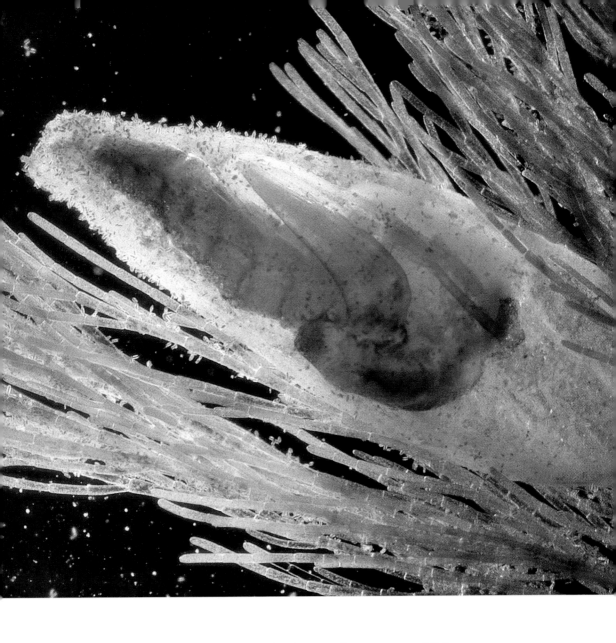

Many insects go through the early stages of life underwater. This is a midge pupa.

Maggot Munchers

What do maggots eat? Many like to munch through decaying plant and animal material, and animal dung is a rich source of food for many different maggots. Others eat plant roots and stems. Young crane flies called leatherjackets, for example, can ruin lawns and shrubberies by nibbling away at the roots of the plants above.

Other flies prefer instead to catch other small animals. New Zealand glowworms are not worms at all. They are the maggots of a type of fly called a fungus gnat (said NAT). New Zealand glowworms live in the mouths of caves, and their bodies glow at night. The light attracts moths and other insects. They become trapped on sticky threads that dangle down from the glowworms' mouths. The glowworms reel in the threads and feast on their struggling victims.

Opposite page: *These may look like strings of pearls. In fact, they are the sticky threads that dangle from the mouths of New Zealand glowworms.*

Feasting Flies

Some adult flies do not feed—they eat all they need when they are maggots and live as adults only long enough to mate. But for flies that do feed, taking in a meal can be a messy business. When an adult housefly lands on something good to eat, it does not take bites from it as a human would. Instead, it dribbles saliva onto the food, which breaks down the food into mushy liquid. The fly then mops up the liquid, using its mouthparts like a sponge.

Many adult flies like to eat sweet, sugary foods, like the nectar of a flower. Flowers produce nectar to tempt insects like flies to visit them. When the flies land, tiny grains of pollen stick to hairs on their bodies. The pollen is carried to other plants by the flies. Plants need to swap pollen with other plants so they can produce seeds. People depend on flies to spread pollen for many important crops. Without certain midges, for example, the plants from which chocolate is made could never grow!

Insect Killers

Not all flies feed on sweet liquids like nectar. Some catch other insects for food. Robber flies are fast-flying hunters. They have very good vision and can snatch up other insects on the wing. Tiny jackal flies also like to eat insects; but rather than catch their own food, they steal it. Jackal flies often live on a robber fly's body. The jackal flies feed on the soup of liquid insect guts that dribbles down the robber fly's head as it feeds.

Some young flies like to eat other insects, too. Bee flies lay their eggs near the entrance to a bee nest. The eggs hatch, and the maggots wriggle inside the nest. There some feed for a time on the supply of pollen and nectar kept by the bee for its young. Most move straight on to feast on the unfortunate young bees.

Opposite page: *Robber flies are ruthless hunters. This one has pounced on another fly feeding on the nectar of a tickseed flower.*

Drinking Blood and Munching Flesh

Nectar doesn't contain all the kinds of food that some flies need to produce healthy eggs. These flies must drink the blood of other animals to help them produce lots of eggs. Female mosquitoes land on the bodies of animals, including humans. They push their sharp mouthparts through the skin and inject a chemical. This chemical stops the blood from clotting (getting thick) and sealing up the hole. That allows the mosquito to keep feeding until it has had its fill. The chemical also makes mosquito bites itch like crazy!

Many adult flies drink blood, but lots of maggots prefer to bite into flesh. Some greenbottle flies, for example, lay their eggs on the bodies of sheep, and the maggots drill their way in.

Here you see blood being drawn up from a person's skin through the mosquito's needlelike mouthparts.

Deadly Diseases

People fear some flies with good reason, since they can pass on diseases. When a mosquito injects saliva into a person as it feeds, it may also inject tiny creatures called plasmodia. They move through the person's blood and cause the deadly disease malaria. Malaria kills more than 2 million people around the world each year.

Another fly, the tsetse fly, is almost as bad. This fly drinks blood from many animals, from frogs and fish to cattle and people. A feeding tsetse fly may pass along another tiny creature in its saliva that causes a deadly disease called sleeping sickness. Another terrible disease, river blindness, is caused by tiny worms that are passed on by blood-sucking black flies. Dead worms build up in people's eyes, making them go blind.

Opposite page: *The tsetse fly carries the creatures that cause the disease sleeping sickness. Here a tsetse fly is cleaning its legs after a meal in which it could have passed on the disease.*

Fighting Crime with Flies

Not all flies cause problems for people. Sometimes they are very helpful. Some flies lay their eggs on dead bodies, and the maggots clean up the flesh by feasting on it as it decays. Different flies lay their eggs at different times depending on how rotten the body is. The young flies then grow at different speeds depending on how warm it is.

When a dead body is found, police scientists look at which types of fly eggs and maggots are on the person's body, and how old the insects are. They also record the temperature. These pieces of information allow the scientists to figure out when the person died. This information is often very important in murder investigations.

The Web of Death

Flies are incredibly common and provide a rich source of food for predators. The best-known fly eaters are spiders. Spiders use their webs to trap flies. Some webs have sticky threads that flies get stuck to; others have fuzzy threads that catch onto the hairs on a fly's body. When a spider catches a fly, it binds it with silk the spider produces. When the fly can no longer move, the spider scuttles in and bites the fly, injecting a fast-acting poison. The spider may eat the fly right away by sucking its juices out, or it may truss it up somewhere safe and tuck in later. Some spiders do not need webs to catch flies. Some jumping spiders can leap up and catch flies in midair.

Enemies Everywhere

Flies are an important food for many animals besides spiders. Frogs and toads use their long, sticky tongues to snatch careless flies as they rest. Praying mantises grab flies with their long, powerful front legs. Underwater fly maggots are eaten by fish. Many birds, such as flycatchers, are also expert fly hunters.

It is not just animals that enjoy flies for supper, though. Some plants eat flies too! These plants need extra foods that the poor soils they live on cannot provide. An insect wandering across the opened snare of a Venus flytrap may touch tiny hairs inside. That triggers the trap, which imprisons the insect. The plant then waits for the insect to die before slowly digesting it. Sundew plants catch flies in a different way. When flies land on a sundew, they become glued to a sticky liquid on the plant's leaves. The leaves then slowly curl up, and the body of the dead fly is broken down to release its foods.

Opposite page:
This unlucky fly has landed inside the jaws of a Venus flytrap plant. In a split second the jaws will snap shut, trapping the fly.

Masters of Disguise

A fly's world is full of hungry predators hunting it. Some flies use sneaky tricks to fool these enemies. Many harmless flies pretend to be other, more dangerous insects. Hover flies and bee flies often have contrasting bands of black and yellow or orange on their bodies. Predators avoid the flies, thinking they are wasps or bees that defend themselves with painful stingers. Pretending to be another animal is called mimicry. Other well-armed animals are also mimicked by flies. One type of fly pretends to be a carpenter ant, while mydas flies mimic spider-hunting wasps. Some flies even imitate jumping spiders.

Some flies use mimicry for more sinister purposes. Thick-headed flies use their beelike disguise to get close to real bees. A thick-headed fly approaches a bee as it gathers food at a flower. The fly then lays its eggs inside the bee's body. When the eggs hatch, they begin to eat away the bee from the inside.

Life Underwater

Most adult flies live on the land, but a few types of female midges live on the surface of rock pools. These strange insects do not have wings. Instead, they row around on the surface with their legs. The young, or larvae, of many flies also grow in water, spending their early days under the surfaces of ponds and rivers.

Like all animals, larvae need to breathe a gas called oxygen to live. How do underwater larvae breathe? Some, like young mosquitoes, breathe at the surface through a tiny tube. They swim up through the water by quickly wriggling their bodies before sinking back down again. A few hover fly larvae have a longer breathing tube that can be extended like the periscope of a submarine! Other flies take oxygen from the water itself.

Opposite page: *The young, or larvae, of many flies live entirely underwater, like this young mosquito. It has just come up to the surface to breathe.*

Supreme Survivors

Opposite page:
Brine flies can take things very, very salty and very, very hot. These brine flies are living in a hot volcanic pool.

Some fly maggots thrive in conditions that would kill any other animal. Underwater midge maggots can tolerate life in the sludge at the bottom of ponds and puddles where there is hardly any oxygen in the water. Some young midges can live at depths of up to 4,460 feet (1,360 meters), deeper than any other insect. Young midges also hold the insect record for exposure to extreme cold; some types can survive a very chilly bath of liquid helium at −454°F (−270°C)!

Another amazingly tough group is the brine flies. As their name suggests, these flies can live in very salty water up to five times saltier than the ocean. Some brine flies live in small pools that often reach temperatures of more than 158°F (70°C), and scientists have discovered that these insects can survive temperatures of up to 392°F (200°C)—hot enough to kill any other animal right away.

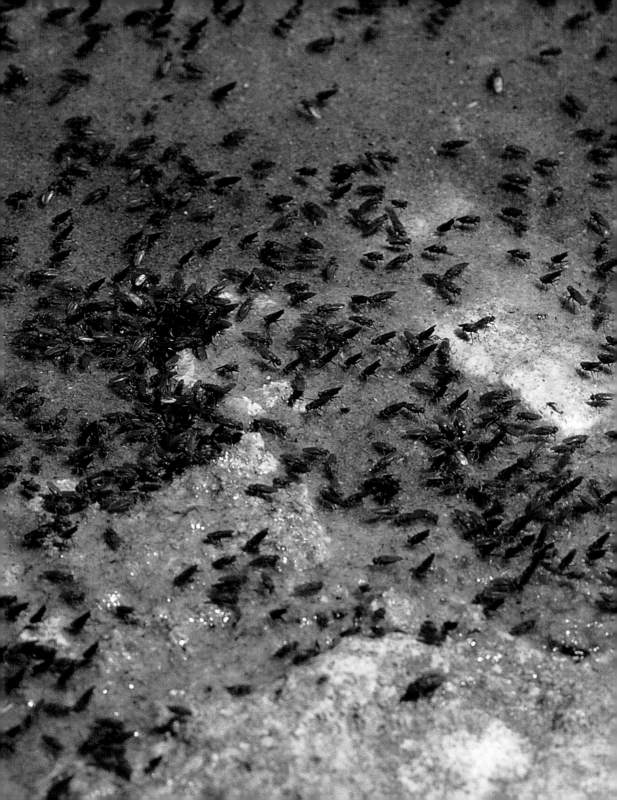

Amazing Rarity

Although many flies are incredibly common, some are very rare indeed. Four strange flies were caught in Bolivia in the early 20th century. They were so different from any other flies that scientists named a new family (large group) of flies for them. None of these broad-headed flies has ever been seen since, and the entire family may have become extinct (died out completely).

Another type of fly lives inside a single crack in a rock on a hill in Kenya—and nowhere else in the world. The flies feed on dung dropped by bats that share their tiny home. North America is also home to an extremely rare fly. The Delhi Sands flower-loving fly lives only in an area of sand dunes near Los Angeles, California. Only 300 or so of these flies survive. They are beautiful, orange-brown insects almost 1.5 inches (3.75 centimeters) long.

Words to Know

Clotting When blood thickens, usually to keep the blood from flowing out of a wound.

Compound eyes The eyes of insects, consisting of up to 30,000 separate eyelets.

Digest To break down food inside the body.

Extinct When all of the animals of a particular species have died, and there are no more left anywhere in the world.

Family A group of different species.

Gills Feathery organs that help insects draw oxygen from water.

Halteres (singular **haltere**) A small pair of tiny little wing stubs that help a fly keep its balance as it flies.

Larva The life stage between an egg and a pupa.

Maggot A young fly.

Mimicry To pretend to be another type of creature, usually to escape predators.

Molt To shed skin.

Nectar The sweet liquid produced by plants.

Predator An animal that eats other animals.

Pupa The life stage between maggot and adult fly.

Species A particular type of animal.

INDEX

Cover Photo: Oxford Scientific Films: Satoshi Kuribayashi
Photo Credits: **Ardea:** Bob Gibbons 7, Steve Hopkin 20, Wardene Weisser 45; **Bruce Coleman:** Janos Jurka 11, Kim Taylor 8, 32; **NHPA:** G. I. Bernard 12, 23, N. A. Callow 16, 27, Stephen Dalton 15, 36/37, 41; **OSF:** 4, 42, David M. Dennis 38, Michael Fogden 24, Brian Kenney 28, Ben Osborne 19; **Still Pictures:** Jean-Claude Teyssier 31.